Inhale/Exile

Bismillahi irRahman irRaheem

Alhamdulillah
I, Mesopotamia,
where two rivers meet
with blood's ink and palm tree dust,
tears and reed flutes sing.

For the keepers of these stories.

Inhale/Exile

Abeer Ameer

Seren is the book imprint of
Poetry Wales Press Ltd.
Suite 6, 4 Derwen Road, Bridgend, Wales, CF31 1LH
www.serenbooks.com
facebook.com/SerenBooks
twitter@SerenBooks

ISBN: 978-1-78172-610-5
ebook: 978-1-78172-611-2

A CIP record for this title is available from the British Library.

The publisher acknowledges the financial assistance of the Books Council of Wales.

Cover painting: 'The day the reed was cut' by Grischa Goldbeck.
grischa.co.uk

Author photograph: Abeer Ameer

The author wishes to acknowledge the award of a place on the Literature Wales
Mentoring Scheme supported by the National Lottery through Arts Council of
Wales for the purpose of completing this work.

Printed in Bembo by Severn, Gloucester.

Contents

The Storyteller 7
Baghdad 1258 CE 8
Four Poets in a Bookshop 9
The Student 11
The Prisoner 12
The Fugitive's Wife *(i) young family* 13
The Lodger, 1968 14
Iraqi Bride in Transit 15
The Fugitive's Wife *(ii) escape* 16
Stigma 17
The Teacher 18
The Journey 19
The Army Doctor 20
The Dentist 21
The Neighbour 22
Kurdish 23
Chemistry 24
Photographer in Halabja, 17th March 1988 25
The Fugitive's Wife *(iii) asylum* 26
The Waiting Groom 27
White Coat 28
Green Ink 30
On Staying Warm 31
Price Tag 32
Bystander 33
The Runner 34
The Postman 35
Finjaan 36
The Fugitive's Wife *(iv) voices* 38
Lost Heads at Firdous Square, Baghdad, 9th April 2003 39
Video Capture 40
Interview with the Hermit 42
The Fugitive's Wife *(v) changes* 44
The Flat Roof 45
The Diver 46
The Fugitive's Wife *(vi) return* 47
The Interpreter 48
The Mechanic 50
The Well 51
Antique Shop 52

Black Car Black Banner   53
Detail   54
A Word I-III   55
What they must know in their hearts   58
The Baker   59
Candlelight   60
Portrait Artist   61
A Scholar of Arabic   62
Learning to Make Iraqi Pickle   63
The Love Letter   64
Hameeda's Prayers   65
The Fugitive's Wife *(viii) metaphor*   66
Passing   67
The Reed Flute and I   68
Yet, He Remembers Baghdad   69
Epilogue   70

Notes   71
Acknowledgements   72

The Storyteller

Aesop had nothing on her. The children gather
on the rooftop level with the heads of Najaf's palm trees,
sit cross-legged ready for stories before bed.
An uneasy weight on her chest; she'd found her youngest
trapping sparrows again.

There was and how much there was…
She tells the story of a beautiful bulbul.
Shiny feathers, bright plumes,
how its song filled the air
until the king ordered it be caught
and caged, kept for his eyes only.
Soon its feathers greyed,
the light in its eyes vanished,
the song in its throat withered.

Her eyes wander to that space,
empty since his fourth birthday.
She continues:

The bulbul's mournful mother
searched everywhere for her child,
unable to eat or sleep.
Both died from sadness.
The king, filled with remorse,
promised to protect all his kingdom's
wildlife
Then he became the kindest,
wisest king on earth.
And they lived a happy life.

She looks to the stars, mutters
When you cling to a thing you love it dies.
Sometimes when you love you must let go…must let go.
Her soft voice trails off. The children focus on the cigarette
in her left hand which balances a tower of ash.
In her right hand, amber prayer beads;
her thumb strokes the top of each before moving it along.
She recites *Al-Fatiha*, scans the sky for the crescent moon.

Baghdad 1258 CE

Blood and ink
met again at the Tigris.
Mongols beheaded many.
Abbasids lost their empire.

That day blood poured
into the Tigris
turning it red
until the next day

when it turned black
from ink of books
from the grand library
torn and dumped

rendering the river
a black mulch
of hadith, science, philosophy.
Little did the Mongols know

that someday soon
the conquerors would themselves
be conquered
by the same black ink.

Four Poets in a Bookshop

In the land of two rivers and hanging gardens,
four poets meet in a bookshop. No one can know.
Portrait of Saddam watches; they hide under the cloak
of Arabic lexicon. They share with one breath
meanings that turn the Master's key
to worlds where Adam was taught the names.

Trees, reborn as pages, witness the names
of four and those gathered to reach the Gardens,
as they escape their locked chests without key.
They are four men who know.
Reading between lines of apocalypse, each strained breath
foretells of beasts with their daggers and cloak

scarring minds and hearts of men by Baathist cloak.
Present are bygone days of Karbala's names
which poets dare to mention under their breath.
Alive and well with the Lord of the Gardens.
Willing to exchange this world for the next, four know
that informants sell to the cruellest bidder for neighbours' key.

Saddam's spies claw to learn of persons key
and clothe their families in mourning cloak.
Three-quarters give eyes, tongues and nails. They know
they must not, to treachery, yield any names.
Silent skin, dipped in acid, bastes in hanging gardens
bearing to keep hidden secrets beyond dissolved breath.

No haste nor waste for ordained beat and breath
nor desire for the iron key
to dust's throne; they dream of other gardens.
Longing only to reunite with the People of the Cloak
and the Most Compassionate through His Names.
Those clinging to ebbing sands of time do not yet know.

The bookshop bears witness to what few mortals know.
Its shelves and books inhale each whispered breath
and all that poetry and scripture, names.
Kerosene warms the last poet. He clutches the bookshop's key,
drinks black tea sugar cannot sweeten and wears a black cloak.
Alone; his companions have already reached the Garden.

Many years after a shroud is his cloak and cancer takes his breath,
the names of seekers are still hidden. Their key is kept buried in the earth
upon which gardens grow, and reed beds and shrines know how to Read.

The Student

Fifteen now, he flies kites with combat strings
of powdered glass to secure victory over Najaf rooftops.
He breeds bulbuls, swims in a caustic soda pool,
runs through cemeteries to be chased by rabid dogs.
Thrill-seeker with the zeal of youth, pompadour hair,

swagger like James Dean – he's a rebel without a cause
until the cause finds him in 1963 – a massacre
he writes about in his school essay.
His bloodline might have ended then,
in a pool of blood,

but for a teacher risking his own bloodline
by not informing on the student traitor.
Returns the essay: *See me after class.*
A quiet word with the boy's father of the hot acid
their Iraqi Jimmy might land them in.

For all their sakes, he's told to keep his head down
a few more years. Soon enough
he'll leave Iraq, study Pharmacy,
listen to Engelbert Humperdinck, Tom Jones,
Malcolm X, Muhammed Ali. He'll hitch-hike

across Ireland with a friend from Hong Kong,
sing *Quando? Quando? Quando?* in a Bradford pub,
work in a dairy in Halifax drinking all the gold-top he can
and learn very quickly
never to give his real name.

The Prisoner

He prays to the one whose existence he denies
just in case he's got it wrong and there is a god.

He finds himself in *Nugrat Al-Salman* prison.
He still denies there is a god.
What brought him here brought those with him
to a tight torture space shared with rats,
comrades and those who still believe there is a god.

Some weep, some are strong, some wail
and some pray there is a god.
Blindfolded, handcuffed numbers,
dragged down corridors and winding staircases.
One can only hope there is a god.

His mother hasn't heard from him.
He's fallen in with communists crying revolution,
says *religion is opium for the masses*, but she knows
there is a god who can deliver him.

She doesn't know his slammed fate in this place
is the same as those staunch in the belief
there is a god and cling to that belief,
despite the taunts that if there is a god,
surely, they would not lie broken-boned,
violet-skinned in the dungeon.

But in the dungeon,
with blood-caked clothes,
poppy eyes, a toothless smile,
he bears witness
in his opium heart
There is God.

The Fugitive's Wife

(i) young family

a short engagement
they marry young

he is already
a turbaned shaykh

before he is shaykh in age
from a good family

shy acceptance
na'am qabiltu

moves to his village
of different customs

and faces
girls don't read here

wife of the shaykh
escorted where she goes

girl and boy
arrive quick

boy often ill
in his first year of life

they still think
that pliers

are only used
to cut chicken wire

The Lodger, 1968

He stays with a Scottish family in Carlisle.
At times they struggle to understand
the young man's accent, his dislike of dogs
and of straining dishes straight from the bowl.

He craves his homeland,
the poetry and birdsong,
his mother's cooking,
his father urging him to read.

An invitation to a party at the hospital
from Carol, the girl with auburn hair,
his classmate in A-level chemistry,
comes just in time.

He finds a crowd gathered around
a bearded man strumming chords on his guitar.
The man sings words which move hearts;
a romantic tone the lodger had not heard before.

Weeks later, the lodger asks about the song.
The girl returns to him with sheet music.
He can't decipher the notes on paper
but that earworm tune still gives him a hum

which keeps him going,
on and on, repeating the line
Don't give up now, little donkey,
Bethlehem's in sight.

Iraqi Bride in Transit

She's nineteen, waits in Charles de Gaulle airport
unsure where to go. She hopes that Groom comes for her soon.

Her first experience of a plane journey hasn't been *Oh là là*.
Far from her Baghdad home, her white suit is not so white now.
It's the first time she wears high heels; she has blisters,
struggles to balance.

She wears her mother's fur coat, a white headscarf,
white clutch bag holds her green passport.
Feels bare without her *abaya*.

Groom waits in Heathrow arrivals. It's 23rd December 1974.
Three flights have arrived from Paris in the last eight hours.
No sign of her.

Iraqi Christians who boarded the same plane
from Baghdad waiting for their New York flight
recognise *she's the bride*, take her to the gate.
Last flight before Christmas.

> *He is pupil. He do drugs.* She rolls her Rs.

Groom's lost hope. It's late.
He gets up, ready to leave Heathrow,
gathers coins to make the international call.
What will he tell her father?

Announcement. Groom is summoned to Immigration.

> *Your wife says you do drugs.*

He realises at that moment he should have taught his bride
the correct English term for *pharmacy student*.

The Fugitive's Wife

(ii) escape

Early days for the iron fist.
First, they came for Communists
then, for the faithful clerics.

Morning exam:
Islamic Jurisprudence.
Saddam's *Mukhabarat*.

They are standing outside
the exam hall, ready to seize
the second-year student
whose name appeared
on the *for execution* list.

The teacher,
unnoticed by those sharpening knives,
with a brisk nod of the head

allowed his student
to climb

       out of the exam hall window

       onto the flat roof

          over the wall
               and

                      run.

The teacher
would need to learn
how
soon enough.

Stigma

He touches
his wedding ring
says the trend
at the time
was each teen
wore a silver ring,
black stone,
on the little finger
of the right hand.
A symbol.
But it left a mark
to mark them out –
a tan-line –
when the *Mukhabarat* came.
It's how they knew,
how they chose.

The Teacher

Parkinson's triad slows his movements,
holds his pill-rolling fingers, his arms,
in cogwheel rigidity. A tremor moves his head.

He once saved a life
by a movement of his head:
a nod to his student

on the *for execution* list
to usher the fugitive
out of the window

before *Mukhabarat* came
through the door.
Soon he faced demands

from Baathist Party officials
to sign a paper
confirming allegiance:

Wallah, cut out my tongue, if you must.
Cut off my fingers one-by-one....
On the run, like his student before him,
bids farewell to those he knows,
those he won't see again in this life.

His voice is whisper-soft now.
His face, masked,
not just by disease.

He sits, prayer beads in his right hand
giving thanks for the movements of his head
in speech only *AlSamee*', the All-Hearing, can hear.

The Journey

she knows she was eighteen

but her mind's blank

how they left the house

arrived at the Iranian border

others tell her how

Saddam's soldiers came late at night

shouting   that   her ancestors   were Persian

that they must   leave Iraq

go back to where they came from

no longer   Trojan horse

fifth column

she can't remember

whether she wore   shoes

to set foot in the land   of distant

ancestors

who spoke in tongues   less guttural

she can't remember   the boundary

or where   they stayed   that first night

they tell her how

families walked barefoot

lost   children   on the way

cold   they were exposed to

so harsh

it's all God's earth

but she can't remember

a single detail

The Army Doctor

Another reluctant soldier.
A right leg injected
with kerosene

swollen and necrotic
as the doctor's own heart.
Amputation of the green-black limb

to save a life
swiftly sent
for *questioning.*

Those who survive
forever marked as cowards
by the removal of one ear.

Other novel ways
remain undiscovered:
a young man who gasps for air,

irreversible lung damage,
inhaling fumes from his car exhaust.
They'll do anything for release

from Saddam's Army.
The doctor wonders whether
he will ever know redemption

as he finds himself caught
between
captive and executioner.

The Dentist

She wants to take a good look at the Najaf dentist
who asked for her hand in marriage.

It's unbecoming,
so she borrows her mother's black *poochiyah*.
Mighty hot, but at least she can see
remain unseen.
She draws her *abaya* over her head,
poised, as if for ballet,
accompanies her cousin
to a dental appointment: a difficult extraction.

She glares,
the office smells of cloves and musk.
He is quiet
works hard to earn a halal wage
silent
but not stern
strong
but not brutish.

He gives minimal post-op instructions,
respectfully tells her cousin not to spit today.
They thank the tooth doctor,
leave relieved.

He thinks about his day:
distally-impacted lower right eight, not too difficult.

*Odd that the slender lady in the poochiyah and black gloves
wore bright pink flip-flops.*

The Neighbour

He spots a fat cat, hears it purr rotundly. Conclusions, which do not involve feline hyperthyroidism or liver ascites, are drawn. He writes a letter to Baathist Party Headquarters:

27th April 1998.

Re: Top Priority Security Report
Salutations of the Struggle!

We have observed that our neighbour on the right side has a cat which has gained weight. We feel this reflects a sudden improvement in the living standards of our neighbour.

In these times of sanctions by aggressors against our most honourable state, cats should not gain weight. One can only conclude the man next door is in receipt of finances from sources external to our noble country, rebellious against The Party and Revolution.

I add that the neighbouring family is known to be poor without a regular source of income. The man does not attend gatherings or celebrations organised by our esteemed leadership. He is not subscribed to membership of any committee. He does not throw rubbish in general disposal. I add that he barbeques frequently. Clearly, this is overwhelming evidence that the man of the house next door is an enemy of The Party and Revolution. Therefore, I urge speedy intervention.

This was written in humble loyalty to The Party and Revolution. We vow to remain vigilant against all threats towards our noble cause.

Forever your colleague in the Struggle. UQJ

The man of the house next door
is nowhere to be found
when the cat has five kittens two weeks later.

Kurdish

Sykes and Picot
forgot
about the existence
of his kind.

It hadn't crossed their minds
that the Kurdish people
have language, food, customs
and a circle dance of their own.

Sweet sixteen. The boy hopes,
as he takes shallow breaths
crouched down
inside the water tank

in the boiler room
of mourning neighbours,
whose own boys and men
had been taken two days earlier,

that Saddam's soldiers
searching houses in Sulaymaniyah
would be so kind
as to forget about him too.

Chemistry

There was chemistry
between them

a spark
so blinding

they were
blinded

under each other's skin
passion undesired

skin blush
blood rush

racing heart
heavy breath

weak knees
paralysis

Mustard Gas.
Sarin.

Panjwin
Sardasht
Al-Faw
Hawizah Marsh
Basrah
Halabja.

At it like rabids.

Cupid looks
the other way.

Photographer in Halabja, 17th March 1988

He shoots everything he sees before him:
families gathered in alleyways,
birds fallen from their nests,
that day in Spring.

In front of steps
the figure of a man rests
wearing Kurdish turban and baggy pants,
a large sash wrapped around his waist,

face down in the dirt,
holding a baby in his arms.
Muted earthy tones around a pink blanket,
a white, glowing face, chin-up to the sky.

The photographer
holds his camera tight
to capture this perfect still life
of the just-dead.

Hands shake as he takes the parting shot:
newborn face towards the camera.
This exposure burns
his right index finger, his retina.

He'll share what the world needs to see
though no image can show the pungent air
thick with sweet apple and bile.
No shadow dark enough.

The Fugitive's Wife

(iii) asylum

Smuggled
to the Kuwaiti border
for the long run
of exile
crossed boundaries
papers
ink blots lives
papers, papers
ink condemns and saves
with each glance
over the shoulder
like the graphs
of *sine* and *cosine*
their paths cross
sometimes

                              flee Iraq

                    to Kuwait

          to Syria

                                        to Iran

          to Syria

                                        to Iran

          to Syria...

                                        ...Canada

The Waiting Groom

Announcement. Groom is summoned to Immigration.
His chest is tight
as his eyes scan the walls and signs.
It is said that men's eyes can hold the ocean,
but he feels like he's drowning.
Until he spots her at the desk.

It's her. The same loveliness.
Just like the first time he saw her
in Baghdad. His eyes fall into hers.

The Immigration Officer's
voice brings him back

Your wife says you do drugs.

An awkwardness he'll know well.

In their bedsit with the leaking roof,
to drip-drip-drops of Sunderland rain,
he'll teach her English. She'll try her best
as both roll their Rs.

She'll mistake Wendy for *windy,* brick for *prick*
be pleased about cheap butter she found to save pennies,
and get hooked on *kammoon* (Cumin) crisps.
He'll teach her the words *lard* and *gammon.*

Years later, their children will invent *Arabish,*
correct their parents' mistranslations:
tap dancing, not lap dancing, incarcerate not castrate
and blunder in the search for home between two rivers.

White Coat

He's newly qualified
but his white coat is not so crisp, not so white.
He drives back from a long shift at *Madinat Saddam al Tibbia*
the six-year-old boy is on his mind
vomiting blood from liver cirrhosis of Hep C.
Sanctions. No cannula, no clean swabs,
no terlipressin, no blood transfusion.
Bled to death in his mother's arms. The doctor's first.

A black four-by-four cut past him at the intersection,
blacked-out windows and eye-watering speed.
He gestures *Why?* with a shrug, outstretched hands
then the car comes to a diagonal halt in front of him.
Four men jump out, parade their bulging pecs and washboard abs,
clench their masseters and glutes.
Perfect for anatomy class, he thinks,
as they drag him from his white Toyota

and beat him. Piercing *Don't you know who we are?*
into his eardrums. Punched in the face, ribs, kidneys, legs
eight fists pound him North, South, East and West.
He spits out blood and remembers the boy,
tries to cover his face, waits for the strikes to stop.
We are bodyguards of the Master, the President.
Wonders if there was anything else he could do,
powerless as the blood pours.

Gunshot. A man sees them, shouts *What's all this?*
The doctor's autonomic nervous system, unable to fight or fly,
Replies: *They are beating me.*
The four turn to face the man who dared intervene.
He has a big black moustache, holds a big gun.
They jump into the four-by-four and speed away.
They know who he is.

The young doctor thanks the stranger,
gets back into his car to drive across the bridge.
Through his left eye, he spots his red-splattered
coat and trousers are wet from the waist down.

His distraught mother sees his bloodied face, his sorry state,
he says that he must have sweat a lot when he was beaten.
He scrubs the bloodstains from his coat; he has work in the morning.
Hopes Mama doesn't realise he'd wet himself.

Green Ink

The thin man in the three-piece suit
is the only one who waits in a queue.
Nobody else cares to take turns.
He comes each year to register deferred entry
for his daughter at Baghdad University, clings
to the hope that dust can settle, things will
get better, and his daughter and her husband can return.
He writes her name, signs in green ink.

At home he settles into his fixing position,
crouched in his white *dishdasha*, glasses to tip of his nose
he fixes irons and kettles, listens to the news on the radio.
At war with brothers in Iran now.
He smokes as he worries. Always wartime it seems.

His daughter in England savours each airmail letter,
the smell of spent matches, deep inhale of green ink
to capture his scent until he visits. It's been years.
She kisses his hands as he gets off the coach from Heathrow.
Kerosene suitcase full of hand-woven loofas, date syrup, bricks of olive
and bay leaf soap, the glass cups and saucers her mother sent.
Black tea as he likes it; heaped sugar, a slice of lemon.
He pours it into the saucer to let it cool, and sips.

Between visits and sips, hairs grey and wars end
and begin. Saddam invades Kuwait.
No contact as the bombs rain on Basra and Baghdad.
Saddam takes revenge on rebels. Stories in parts.
She hears he's passed and mourns her father though he lives.
Six months. She doesn't know until crossed lines
transmit the echo of his voice. Soon, the same unsettled dust
blocks his coronary arteries. His fountain pen dries,
his pocket watch stops telling time. Exhale.
A portrait of Saddam facing his hospital bed.

On Staying Warm

After Zeina Hashem Beck

Her groom is a fan of Um Kulthum,
insists on explaining each word of the songs,
says *Um Kulthum sings to God.*
Each song lasts at least an hour.
She doesn't get it; it's not music one can dance to.

Kawkab always takes so long to get the words out.
Dark glasses, silk handkerchief in her right hand.
Full orchestra behind her as the crowd sways *Allah, Allah.*
Many lost their minds to become the *Majnun* of her *Layla.*

The bride humours her groom, smiles,
wishes the lyrical dissection would end quick.
She doesn't say she prefers
Abdul-Haleem Hafez, Fayruz, the Bee Gees.
They are newly-weds after all.

She's in a cold land, her groom's thermals
not enough to keep her warm.
She wants to go back to where they came from.
She writes letters to her sisters each day
wonders when she'll receive an airmail envelope
addressed to her in Iraqi ink. The smell of home.

She doesn't know that in years to come
she'll drive a beige Honda with faulty carburettor
that will stall on each school run.
As the tape stops and starts
she'll keep going, playing sides A and B
of Um Kulthum on repeat to stay warm.
Translate and explain every song
word for word
to each of her five children.

Price Tag

On 12th May 1996, Madeleine Albright gave a television interview with
60 minutes. Leslie Stahl, speaking of US sanctions against Iraq, asks if the
price is worth it.

She didn't twitch, deny or confirm it
that half a million children had died.
But the price, we think, the price is worth it.

More than the dead children of Hiroshima; all heard it.
I think this is a very hard choice said Madeleine Albright.
She didn't twitch, deny or confirm it.

A sorry subject. She didn't skirt it.
Most affected: babies and under-fives.
But the price, we think, the price is worth it.

Starving child and mother who birthed it,
nursing mothers' milk all dried.
She didn't twitch, deny or confirm it.

I think this is a very hard choice. Far from perfect.
When a miniature grave's the only place to hide.
She didn't twitch, deny or confirm it.
But the price, we think, the price is worth it.

Bystander

Also known as *collateral damage*.
The usual story for his type:
minding his own business
tending to his pomelos and pomegranates
and watering his carnations. His granddaughter watches
as he spreads fig leaf sap to cure his psoriasis.

Guided missiles
don't show the usual signs of guidance.
They don't shout *Hallelujah*,
they don't clap in praise of the Lord
and they don't quietly come seeking
a Bodhi tree under which to sit cross-legged
to reach Enlightenment.

They do bring with them
an almighty blast of fire and light.
For eons
people speak of them in many tongues
and warn of the preceding hum
leaving bystanders
in eternal stand-by.

The Runner

Not sure when she hit the wall;
the beginning of unending
unfolds to full halt.

Alone with faces and sounds she knows.
A sea of heads and limbs around her
coloured tops drum lightheaded.

Dry mouth. She's off pace. Weak
with sore calves and quads.
Shoes and legs everywhere.

Her scarf has slipped back,
hair clings to her brow. There is no sound.
She holds her *abaya* in her teeth.

She's lost her right shoe, her left hand.
Sweat drips from her ears, she tastes blood,
feels a limp arm around her neck.

She looks ahead, sees green birds,
faces asleep without breath.
Eyes she looked into moments before
glazed.

The Postman

When he handed
the brown envelope with typed address
to Abu Shihab, father of five doctors,
he knew it wasn't good news.

Two were absent from their shifts yesterday.
Forbidden from taking sick days or annual leave
they were summoned by the government
to answer for their crime.

Serious trouble
unless they had already died
in which case the lesser punishments
for not informing the state immediately.

Abu Shihab had not slept for days,
knowing two of his sons had already embarked
on a journey to escape Iraq by road to Jordan
with passports stating they were merchants, not doctors.

An unknown fate in another land loyal to Abu Uday.
Abu Shihab read the summons, forehead furrowed,
folded the letter, put it back in the envelope,
returned it to the postman.

The postman understood. For weeks he'd repeat to his superior
Wallah, Wallah, the house was empty again.
He risked his everything
for Abu Shihab and the three sons left.

Forever to be known as
Hero, Man of Honour,
and World's Worst Postman.

Finjaan

Read the finjaan for us, Um Ali
the women of Baghdad used to say.
Days when delicate cups filled with black coffee
were offered more often in joy than sorrow.

In joy, coffee is sweetened
and scented with cardamom,
served with pastries; *klaicha* of dates
or rosewater pistachios.

In sorrow, taste grief's bitterness with the host
which no sugar can sweeten
and inhale the cigarette smoke
with which it is served.

When the women gathered
to hear Um Ali on lighter days,
she always accepted.
The ladies drank bittersweet

until the thickness gathered at the bottom
of the cup without handles,
and turned it over,
hopeful for a blessed future.

Um Ali loved to gaze upon the dark hieroglyphs
on the walls of the cup. Fish, snakes, horses
and letters told her secrets
in tongues only she could understand.

Ibsumee Um Ali would say.
The drinker eagerly pressed her right thumb
into the coffee sludge, hoping that the harder
she pressed, better moons would appear.

But Um Ali does not read now.
When women request her foretelling
she smiles, dismisses it as superstition,
jokes that Jinn don't talk to her anymore.

Those who know Um Ali know.
They remember from that last time:
the creases in her forehead,
the constriction of her pupils,

the quake in her voice.
She will never read again.
No one can bear
to know the future here.

The Fugitive's Wife

(iv) voices

Now *safe* she could not let herself
hear the only voices
which wash away memories
of pliers and electric cable.

*Do not give real names
despite being told you are safe now.
Mukhabarat are everywhere.
Beware what you tell the children.*

She wonders how survival
had become undesirable.

*Your mother had a lymphoma.
Your father had a stroke.
They came for your brother.
Inna Lillah wa Inna Ilayhi Rajioon.*

She overheard
another exile let it slip
a year too late
to pray *salat alwahsha.*

*Do not trust
other exiles.
Safety and Freedom
are not real.*

Insomnia
replays the final exchange:
her eyes and words
must not betray the fact
that there were smugglers
waiting for her
at the border with Kuwait.

Lost Heads at Firdous Square, Baghdad, 9th April 2003

I	II	III
Sculptor	**Marine**	**Citizen**

He watches in disbelief	As shoes and sandals fly	Destruction in mind
the bronze statue	at the head	sledgehammer at plinth
he fashioned	willing it to come to life	Rage. Rage
for Saddam	a ladder is raised, a crane	chain noosed at neck
in slow motion	Marine wipes stars, stripes	Years' desire to avenge
torn down	over bronze brow	blood of martyrs many
conquered	cheering crowd silent	unleashed
realisation	quickly replaced	spilled out
sorrow for time gone	to raise an Iraqi flag	over 5 metres of bronze
That photograph	It was just a moment	Sculpture crash to earth
He can't stand straight	the whole world saw	Firdous Square
Heartache bends back	Humvee & tanks ahead	All aim at that face
portraits and art pieces	watch and wait.	The head is first prize
plush chairs, gold & red	Perfect sniper bait	kicked & dragged
around the one	in joyful crowds.	down streets of Baghdad
who feels dishonour	This day has been	Shoe-throwers celebrate
looting his home.	peaceful so far	gun-toting for treasure
Those days are gone.	*100% justified.*	*Free at last.*

Years & souls have passed	He remembers	Mourns fleeting hope
See! The war continues	the carnage & the fallen	lost forever to dust.

Video Capture

After eight months on the run, Saddam Hussein, former president of Iraq, was captured on 14th December 2003.

I

Ace of Spades found in a hole
six feet deep, eight feet wide.
A muddy orange grove
close to the Tigris
headquarters for the latest
assassinations and car bombs.

Iftah femmek they say.
Saddam opens his mouth as they search
his hair, beard, and molars
for weapons of mass destruction.

II

Had they got hold of him, in one of his palaces
or his mosque decorated with the image of his fingerprint
he would have met a fate like that the future held for Gaddafi;
lynched. Unquenched thirst.

One wonders whether Saddam too would have begged
like Gaddafi did in his final moments:
Bloody face, kicked and punched.
Back bent double to expel his pleading voice *haram alaykum*
        shuffling noises to a blur.
                Surrounded.
Video pauses from the rolling footage.
Maybe for time to crush a rib, rip a limb.
Clear signs of torture when the film starts rolling again.

        Dead body in an ambulance. Shot in the head, abdomen.
Cameraman cannot suppress
the joy of destroyed men recording revenge.

III

Defence team walkouts
to a hail of bullets and shootouts
boycott proceedings.

Dujail witnesses, interviews
and videos of the mass graves,
skulls, extracted teeth and nails
cracked bones rip hearts out.

Footage blacked out.
'Combative' Saddam demands firing squad
not hanging as a common criminal.

His most recent lawyer an *American stooge.*
Viewers hear his rallying cries:
insurgency until liberation.

Guilty verdict. Death by Hanging.
Other Crimes Against Humanity not investigated.

IV

Hanging Day 30th December 2006, 6am.
Official reports of 'submissive' Ace of Spades.
Three masked guards.

A black scarf around his neck
then the noose.
He refuses the hood.

He goads emboldened countrymen as they jeer
Muqtada! Muqtada!

Did not finish proclaiming the *Shahada*
before the drop.

Interview with the Hermit

In Al-Numaniyah province, a town known for violent death
of saints and would-be prophets, Jawad holds a matchbox.
He opens it to show fifteen adult teeth he lost during the years
he lived level with martyrs of the town. He points to the ground
which kept the secret of his underground exile; his hermit home.
On Saddam's 'execution' list. He, his mother, and brother in prayer

for guidance. They were shown the answer to the *Istikhara* prayer
in the same dream: the path to avoid death
at Baathist hands began with steps to the basement of their home.
That he must live in a furnace-sized box,
two and a half metres by three-quarters, two metres underground.
Overnight they built a wall in the basement. At twenty-seven years

of age, he had no idea that, for the next twenty-one years
and four months, he wouldn't face Mecca straight in prayer,
he'd listen to radio through headphones. His life underground.
Osteomalacia wolfed bones, teased out teeth, as his sister coughed a TB death
upstairs. His mother wept at her dead daughter's carriage box,
knowledge of a buried-alive son kept mourners away from home.

Frequented by the dead and hiding the living, this home
remained a paradise at his mother's feet. Days stretched to years.
When her eldest son returned to her from Iran's border in a box
her heart was pushed into failure. Alive only by secrets and prayer.
He heard the doctor warn them to expect the Angel of Death
within hours. He took water from the well he'd dug in the ground

for ablution, begged God to save her. Alive again to stand ground
when neighbours sought to extend their home
closer to her land. *No matter how close to neighbours, death
is always closer.* Neighbours couldn't understand, tried to dig again; years
of dust were blown through the air vent to the choked prayer
of the man who could only reach out to touch the holy box.

Mother shrieks; digging stops. He takes the Quran from its box,
kisses the worn pages, rests his forehead upon the ground
uttering words only heard by ants and God; an earnest prayer
Ya Allah, I only have you. Radio announces *freedom* from a home
hidden from sunlight for twenty-one years.
Allahu Akbar from the throat which had just tasted death.

He shows a milk tooth in a trinket box. *Before my mother's death,
I married and was blessed with a son. He's six years old.* He smiles, sweeps
the ground to uncover the vent to his old home, prostrates in
                                                    a prayer of thanks.

The Fugitive's Wife

(v) changes

Powers

over   lines

       in   the   sands

          drawn   and   quartered

     by   quiet

    oiled

           and

                bloody hands

The Flat Roof

Wall surrounds the yard
level with palm tree heads

metal bedframes wait
for cool mattresses

crisp air at dusk
fresh cotton sheets

bestooga pickle jars
tomato paste sundried

swifts and bats in flight
birdsong and Apache hum

The statue topples
in Firdaus Square

neighbours, friends
wrong sect here

militias come
pick families

one by one.
Cleanse the place.

Bullet-filled gates.
A signal to leave.

Counted among
the lucky ones.

The Diver

It's no coincidence that he was born in March:
Pisces, romantic who loves to swim,
he's been called by the government for his services again.

He keeps coming back, no matter how bad it gets.
He loves the rivers and oceans. Despite no-go zones,
barriers and metal nets, he can't help but return to the Tigris,

and marvel at how she can give and take,
bend and curve, kiss the Euphrates at the Marshes,
cry at what they hold.

Today he holds his breath
in his hands, feels the skin-to-skin connection
as he finds another body. This time with no head.

He loosens it from the Tigris tangles.
Baghdad 2007 has been difficult.
The man with no head

will be buried tomorrow in an unmarked grave
if no family comes for him.
Another lonely *Janaza* prayer.

Dragged up, it shows hands tied behind the bullet-ridden back.
The diver will probably find the family,
or head, downstream somewhere.

The diver's own family wants to leave Iraq.
They say he's a dreamer, tell him there is no hope left,
no point in holding his breath hoping for peace.

But he knows the Tigris has been black and red,
seen much worse than this yet forgives.
Besides, he says, *I can hold my breath for a   very   long   time.*

The Fugitive's Wife

(vi) return

generations of fugitives
fulfilling the dream

come together
under one roof

babies
children
parents
grandparents

she doubts she'll ever learn
how to
set the generator
carry the gas cylinders
light the hob with matches
without burning fingers
eyebrows
or incinerating themselves
and the house
stay out of view
recognise suicide bombers
militia members
crooked personnel
insurgent rebels

and win the hearts and minds
of folk suspicious of foreigners

in this alien land
called *home*

The Interpreter (*Alif* to *Thaa*)

Alif ا

Dhiyaa Mahmoud Abdullah Yaqoub
has an English degree from Basra University,
translates for the British Army.
They call him Dave.

He tells his parents he sells ice-cream at the base.
He swaps his *dishdasha* for jeans,
wears balaclava to work, charmer dodges IEDs
and takes bullets for the lads. Money's good if he lives.

He hopes Britain will save Iraq
from men who use scripture to sell war:
those who exhort to *cleanse, purify,*
reclaim glory of the empire,
make the nation great again.

They have no use
for the dozen Arabic words for Love,
or the ninety-nine names for God who is greater.
Even *Al-Fatiha* won't open their hearts.

Baa ب

He turns to the West for guidance.
That's why the unnamed voice
on his phone calls him *traitor, apostate,*
spits that he'll be slaughtered like the dog he is,
that they'll slit throats, burn the womb that bore him.

His name, his voice, on the kill list.

He's not sure he still believes
in the Loving One Who guides him to tie his camel
but after three years of application forms
Alhamdulillah
he's granted asylum to the United Kingdom.

Taa ت

The last time he hears his mother's voice
she calls him the light of her eyes,
her heart,
her after-liver,
says she'll put him on her head,
go to sacrifice for him,
that his leaving burst her gall-bladder
and dragged her soul from her body.

What he wouldn't give to kiss
the paradise under her feet now.

Translation to English
is too dry to taste the spoken blood
which flows through guttural throats.
No matter how much rain falls in England.

Thaa ث

He thirsts
for the dusty air,
the cockerels and *athan*
calling sleepers to wake up and pray,
the bulbuls which remind him
that the garden needs watering.

He blames the cold in his chest on British weather,
doesn't understand why
his new neighbours don't like him.

They too look back on former glories,
scream at Dave to go back to where he came from.

The Mechanic

He flicks through the photos in his album
points out a grinning man, thick moustache.
He helped me cut down to three cigarettes a day.

The one he sees at every turn
on the ground with half his head blown off.
On each slam of a car bonnet
having fixed brakes and belts

door shut and metal crash
of mother's wails;
he's just returned the body
again
again
again

but at least there was something
to recite *janaza* over.
Every Thursday afternoon
he carries watermelons for his uncle

his ribs taste the khaki cracks
lifting bullet-holed bodies,
broken backs;
brothers who never walked again.

At night when others sleep
he steps out into the darkness

feels the fallen bodies under his feet
hears gunfire and dogs barking,

He smells the burning hair and flesh
through the jasmine-scented air of the garden.

The Well

Fled Baghdad
in the Desert Storm
returned to find thirsty taps
in days when no news is bad news.

The man with wife and six children
walked on the road to Baghdad
dreamt that coming home would mean
he could give each one

more than a capful of water
from more than one 500ml bottle.
The children can't understand
why they are tired of adventures.

He has dug the dead earth many times before
but this is the first time
he digs for water
the first time he digs for life.

There has been running water
for some years now
but they keep the well
just in case.

Antique Shop

Her eye falls to a dusty corner at the back
past carved walnut trays and brass cup dew.
Past craft worked into brooches, silver medals
tapped into shape. Old souls poured into moulds.

She asks to see the oil lamp out of reach, top shelf.
The shopkeeper forgot its presence, recalls its story.
He rubs off the dust, blows into the air
tells her it's French from the 1930s.

She strokes the turquoise oil font
and polishes the chimney glass.
She turns the brass wick-raising dial,
watches threads of a new wick emerge in the centre.

She's taken back to that space,
that cave near the stairs back home.
They're huddled together, hunchbacked
far from all windows and furniture.

She hears her aunt's muffled whimpers between sirens and quakes,
as she watches the flame flicker, those *Jinns'* dancing shadows.
Mama repeats the Verse of the Throne and all the litanies she knows;
solemn recitation under the kerosene breath they share.

She asks the antique dealer how much for the lamp.
In no mood to bargain, she'll pay the asking price.
These days, the air is thick with *never again*
but things are just like they used to be.

Black Car Black Banner

Monday, fifth of March.
Year two thousand and seven.
Al-Mutanabbi Street.
Papers bound neat on pavement.
Scholars' ink district.

'Ala baab Allah:
They stand at God's threshold
for some lawful bread.
Sell books, pens, perfume.
Market morning has broken.

Callers and their wares.
Leblebee. Leblebee:
chickpeas with lemon
Sibah. Sibah: prayer beads.
Recite the ninety-nine names.

Shahbandar Cafe.
Four sons, one grandson.
Black car passes. Explosion.
Burning pages everywhere.
He shuts his eyes forever.

Thirty dead, one hundred hurt.
Now, year two thousand and eight.
Black banner, yellow writing.
Charred bundles of paper gone.
Shahbandar Martyrs' Cafe.

Al-Fatiha. Al-Fatiha.

Detail

On 3rd July 2016, a few minutes after midnight, a suicide truck-bomb targeted the Al-Hadi shopping mall in the Karrada district of Baghdad. It was busy with families shopping for the end of Ramadan. Over three hundred and forty civilians were killed and hundreds more injured.

father
his son's

They won't say   found
amongst
friends
a flat roof
They won't say

fourteen-year-old

missing
They won't say
ringtone
Eid clothes
three days early

They won't say   photo ID
glasses

Germany score
found

They won't say

his parents

They don't know how long it took

A Word

I

scrabble in grey matter
search
shine a torch
for a link between
the tip of the tongue
and the body of the larynx
vocal cords stretched
to umbilical chords
rack the brain
on the rack
of understanding

to find a word to convey
and erase
from existence.

II

what is the word to describe
when you go to
a birthday party
graduation
wedding

and see
his face
at each doorway,
each window,
each wall?

when you do not see
clocks in the room with strip lighting

but hear the seconds tick
as the barking cough next door

scratches your own palate?

when the words
form a tumour in your throat
but do not make a sound?

when you kiss
the rosy cheek of the future
it turns ashen grey
burning itself into
your lips and retina?

when survivor's guilt
rips the aorta in two?

III

If that word were

found
known
and written

with a scratchy fountain pen
almost parched of ink
ripping the tissue paper
at each stroke
like the ripping of a butterfly's wings
or the snag of a broken nail
pulling at threads of a shroud

with each creak
of the metacarpal-phalangeal
and interphalangeal joints
eroded with arthritis
holding the pen

and the word
were to be set alight
engulfed by flames

its ash dissolved in acid
smoke dispersed
so that particles of charred tissue paper
boiled ink

are overwhelmed
by fresh air

would breathing be easier?

would there be closure?

What they must know in their hearts

after Dontë Collins

to still call on a God who won't directly respond,
to receive an answer they can't question, can't bargain with.

No changing decree of One unconfined. Alpha, Omega; a
God both Manifest and Hidden, known by each name.

It's so strange, so peculiar. No?
In each prayer their hearts beat, they breathe longer

for something they know from *AlHayy,* the Ever-Living.

The Baker

The baker kneads and comforts the dough to make this day's bread
Pats it to a diamond eye, pinches both ends, to shape this day's bread.

Athan calls to each mourner that they've been blessed
By the God who is always greater, who gave this day's bread.

Inner and outer canthi dry of tears the baker sheds.
She loved samoon. From his crushed airway, this day's bread.

Dormant seed once breathed as wheat, died to give grain's dust.
His hands knock it back to rise again, this day's bread.

His fingertips flatten each ball of dough, newborn soft,
Palms lay each one to rest in burning clay, this day's bread.

It puffs up like chests of angry men, is wrapped in white cloth to stay warm.
Broken just like the breaker, it sighs steam of age, this day's bread.

Opens to the oath of mint and holy basil. The baker knows
It's perfumed with the nectar of each sealed fate – this day's bread.

Candlelight

She
was
candlelight
once
but her light
slipped away
as the wax melted
it drowned
the struggling wick
killing
the flickering flame
even moths ignore her now
their paper wings safe
from being singed
there is nothing left of her
but a puddle of cooling wax
a stub of black wick
and mourning
charred
vapour

.

.

.

Twilight he broke her
at the vigil by handing
her a tealight candle.
Her eyes broke him
the moment the candle
was lit.

Portrait Artist

She draws the same photo
through strokes of charcoal,
strengthens lines to hold him close.
Sketching mistakes are easier to erase,

yet she still can't get a true likeness:
the soul who took every room with him
and left each chamber of her heart
empty.

Just like when his mobile ringtone
became the means to find him
and his friends, it is as if he knew
how this photograph would be used

three weeks shy of his fifteenth birthday.
He wears a black T-shirt,
his fringe flipped to the left,
the lighter part of his hair spiked-up.

He looks past the camera,
gives a suitably solemn smile for the image
to accompany the poems and eulogies
in each room.

The blue and green balloons behind him
have been obscured since that day
by black banners and white prayers.
She knows she'll always feel the heavy waves

as she tries to capture his eyes, the curves of his face.
She draws a portrait of shadows and shapes of carbon
in a landscape now without colour.
Even without the photo, she sees his face at every turn.

A Scholar of Arabic

A scholar of Arabic unable to sleep
beats out rhyme and *wazn*,
elegy for a prisoner
on Saddam's Death Row.

The least he can do as prison guard,
though he never shares,
unless wishing
to write his own.

He knows they knew
as those facing death do
that he mourns them when he can't sleep
and greets them when he can.

He chain-smokes to avoid talking,
marries late,
weeps as often
as he avoids death.

Years later he finds himself
writing another elegy,
this time for the smiling boy,
who could not escape the burning mall.

Learning to Make Iraqi Pickle

He knows it won't be the same
but still watches the video on repeat.

He'll rewind and pause,

write instructions in his green book,
loosen the cobwebs of his Arabic hand.

Eleven minutes and eighteen seconds;
a video in Arabic that lasts four hours.

Play
     rewind
          pause
               rewind
          pause.

He watches as she holds and slices
turnips, cauliflower and cucumber.

Her soft voice. The same accent.
Any type of vinegar she says. She must also be an exile.

Each time she pours, like his mother,
she says *Bismillah*.

He closes his eyes, hears the birds at sunset,
smells baked *samoon* bread, fried aubergine.

On his tongue, the sour sweet of cucumber,
warm from the *bestooga* jar on the flat roof.

The Love Letter

After Muhammed Mahdi Al-Jawahiri

Beloved stranger, upon your hills be peace.
And your birds and your moons and two rivers.
There is such deep sorrow in your song of praise;
beneath your clays and earths, the bodies of lovers.
Blessed are their tongues which spoke truth through pain,
their dry throats, once filled with dust, now Light. Gardens
live their sweetness, feed each date and fig in God's names.
Blessed be your reedbeds and palm trees, your curves and marshes.

Since the grief you tasted, may you breathe the healing sought.
May goodness flow from you, be solace for those who seek.
Blessed be your skins and inks. The wisdom prophets taught
imbibe light though each leaf, each track, each breeze.
Homeland. Cradle. Peace be upon you. Be whole.
Be honoured. Be open. Be still. Peace for all.

Hameeda's Prayers

Her father, Grand Shaykh, was a scholar of the Tradition.
He spent little time on worldly matters. She had one
older brother, six younger siblings. Each dawn her father was seen
walking to Imam Ali's shrine, to teach Quran. In his final hour,
he asked if it was yet time to pray.

In those days, when it was noon, *Dhuhr* time to pray,
scholars wore their turbans – black, white or green, by tradition;
marks of learning and lineage – walked to the shrine. The hour
her father died, her older brother turned eighteen. He said everyone
in Najaf, masses from afar, students in coloured turbans, were seen

at the afternoon of his burial. Her father passed from the Seen
world to the Unseen world, humble as he came. She would pray
for protection of *Al-Qadir, Al-Ahad*, the All-Powerful, the One,
from the cellar's scorpions as she collects melons. The tradition:
to honour guests and visit the shrine. An angel came the hour

her brother's best friend visited; a glance filled his heart that hour.
Shy, smitten, he told his curly-haired sisters, he'd just seen
her long, straight hair; her abaya slipped as she swept. Tradition:
his father asked for her hand. She cut hair, curled for the wedding. *Pray
it grows back quickly. A good time for supplication is dusk.* One

would hear her repeat litanies her father taught, and *Al-Fatiha*; the one
of seven verses. They were blessed with seven children. The Hour
always on her mind. Brothers flee; sons taken; wars grip home; she prays.
Ayat Al-Kursi, prostrates nightly for closeness to God. She's seen
wandering in the house, fingers beads, thankful for tradition.

Each hour spent in worship of the One. A widow, she starts a
new tradition: she's seen taking ablutions, asking grandchildren,
    great-grandchildren: *Did I pray? Did anyone see me pray?*

The Fugitive's Wife

(vii) metaphor

From dawn until dusk
from dusk until dawn
they have been
strangers running

stop to catch breath
sometimes
the only respite
of calm

she sits in the Critical Care Unit
rudimentary
the word *Care* out of place
waits for her husband

to leave an induced coma
a narrow escape
with each machine beep
feels the crack of her own heart

her own arteries
hardened with worry
she asks herself
and *Al-Aleem*, the All-Knowing,

whether it was just
the inevitability of life

of clay upon clay
of dust upon dust.

Passing

After Qays ibn Al-Mulawwah

Passing the dwellings, she'll trace the streets,
derelict sands and remains of walls.
She kisses them not for the walls but the breeze
of those once here whom she adores.

She stands at half-mast of her five feet tall
held up by the promise *with hardship comes ease,*
She breathes jasmine and dust they inhaled before.
Passing the dwellings, she'll trace the streets

in mourning that her heart still beats.
She holds her son's shirt, her mother's prayer shawl,
finds faces in shadows; she's clothed in black sheets.
Derelict sands and remains of walls

echo ululations and smacks from footballs.
Athan calls *God is greater* in desert heat,
spread scent left in stones, breathe sighs with all.
She kisses them not for the walls but the breeze.

She's not alone wandering while others sleep;
shadows and bats share dawn and nightfall.
She sees names in rocks, hears moons speak
of those once here, whom she adores.

She knows all but *Al-Hayy* shall fade and fall;
that life and death in decreed cycles must meet.
Pomegranates and figs from each market stall
taste only of grief, yet greet her with *Peace,*
passing the dwellings.

The Reed Flute and I

after Mawlana Jalaluddin Rumi

As the reed flute sings you weep your sorrow;
your heart still beats in the place you left. The weight
of your yesterdays that were once tomorrows
halves you, just like the day the reed was cut
pulled from its bed, carved to carry the breath
of the carver to ears held far. Its inhale
is your exhale; as if straight from your own chest.
Its wails redden your eyes. Its larynx speaks your exile.

The same parting that split the reed from its bed
brings you together and you can't know until
you've always known; when they said farewell, you bled
so long, knowing you would not fare well, and still
only long for the place your heart comes from.
Reading in tongues; all music yearns for home.

Yet, He Remembers Baghdad

After Edward Thomas

He has dementia, yet he remembers Baghdad.
Hippocampus shrunken, he forgets other names.
The time of his wife's final breath is engraved
yet he forgets who else went and who came.

He folds tissues. He clears his throat.
The aged epiglottis can't tell water from air.
He saves newspapers and empty crisp packets.
His hearing aid whistles as he sighs and stares.

Ink on his fingers, he annotates photographs
to remind himself and others who he is.
Writing his name on each black and white image,
he forgets which of the five sons he lives with.

He tightens a robe around his shadowed form
quoting Jawahiri's lines *two rivers and blessed sands.*
As rain taps the window, he yearns for the dusty sky
where clocks tick loud: his own promised land.

Epilogue

Bullet rounds and birdsong hang in the air
as she stirs the chickpea and meat stew *Timen wa Qeema.*

Aluminium pots almost large enough to hold her sorrow.
The last time her calloused hands stirred pots this big

was to fulfil an oath for *Ashura.* Now she gifts
the rewards of her offering for her son

Al-Marhoom – he who is shown mercy.
One year tomorrow.

Today, her rough skin is used
to the cooking fire's heat

immune to blisters and charring;
numb as she wishes her heart would be.

The scent of dried limes and seven spices
fills the streets of Najaf;

cardamom suspends in the spaces
between air's molecules

sharing sky's gaps with jasmine and rose,
kerosene and camphor.

She mutters prayers to *Al-Rafi'* that one day
a sweet aroma will rise from her kitchen

to fill the streets with rosewater, pistachios
a saffron rice pudding dew.

Though she's blind now,
her inner eye beholds celebration.

Notes

Al-Fatiha: literally means The Opener and is the first chapter of the Qur'an. Seven verses recited many times a day during daily prayers. Recited for blessings, for healing, beginning something new and for those who have passed away. Considered to be a summary of themes within the Quran.

Alhamdulillah: All praise and thanks belongs to God.

Alif, Baa, Taa, Thaa: The first four letters of the Arabic alphabet.

Athan: The call to prayer.

Bismillahi irRahman irRaheem: In the Name of God, Most Gracious, Most Kind. Can be shortened to *Bismillah*, meaning In the Name of God.

Inna Lillah wa Inna Ilayhi Rajioon: Indeed, to God we belong and truly to Him we shall return.

Istikhara Prayer: A prayer for guidance.

Janaza: Muslim funeral prayer before burial.

Little Donkey: A popular Christmas carol written by Eric Boswell.

Majnun: Crazy or madman. *Layla*: Arabic girls' name meaning night.
Majnun Layla: Reference to seventh century story about Arabic poet *Qays ibn al-Mulawwah* who fell in love with Layla. Her father forbade their marriage. Qays was bereft and exiled himself to the wilderness to compose love poems. He became known as *Majnun Layla*: Madman of Layla.

Muhammed Mahdi Al-Jawahiri: An Iraqi poet, considered one of the greatest Arabian poets of the twentieth century. He died in exile in Syria in 1997.

Mukhabarat: Intelligence Service.

Ninety-nine names of God in Islam (*Allah* in Arabic): the names of God revealed in the Quran.

Salat alwahsha: A prayer performed for the deceased on the first night after burial.

Shaykh: Can mean religious scholar or man of advanced age.

Sykes-Picot Agreement; officially *Asia Minor Agreement*: a secret agreement between Mark Sykes (Britain) and François Georges-Picot (France) in 1916, defining spheres of influence and control of Asia Minor.

There was and how much there was: Literal translation of Arabic equivalent of Once upon a time.

Um Kulthum: Famous Egyptian singer (d.1975) known as *Kawkab Al-Sharq* literally meaning Planet of the East, often translated as Star of the East.

Wallah: An oath meaning By God.

71

Acknowledgements

Thanks to the editors of the following publications for first giving these poems (or their earlier versions) a home: *Acumen, Atrium, Envoi, The High Window, The Interpreter's House, Long Poem Magazine, LossLit Magazine, Magma, New Welsh Review, Planet, Poetry Wales, Prole, The Rialto, Tears in the Fence* and *Voices Anthology.*

The Reed Flute and I was commended in the Troubadour Poetry Prize 2020. Many thanks to the judges Mark Doty and Mona Arshi.

Many thanks to my first poetry teachers who gave me a glimpse of what could be: Emma Beynon, Christina Thatcher and Amanda Rackstraw. Thanks to Barakah Blue who introduced me to Rumi's poem *The Lament of the Reed Flute.*

To the wonderful staff at Literature Wales for awarding me a spot on the Mentoring scheme and putting me in touch with the bees knees that is mentor extraordinaire, Katherine Stansfield: Thank you. Thank you to those who encouraged me to share my work when I first started writing: *Roath Writers, First Thursday* and *Where I'm Coming From.*

I'm ever grateful to friends who have read these poems and nudged me in the right direction for improvement and fine-tuning: whose works have inspired my own writing, and who have kindly offered support and helped me tremendously: Katherine Stansfield, Amanda Rackstraw, Leona Medlin, David Forster-Morgan, Stephen Payne, Helen McSherry, Heather Trickey, Rachel Carney and Gillian Clarke. Many thanks to my wonderful friends at The Spoke: Elizabeth Parker, Bob Walton and Claire Williamson for their support and encouragement.

Many thanks to the very lovely Amy Wack for her tireless support, for believing in these poems and humouring me when I use words like 'rotundly'. Huge thank you to all the good folk at Seren for their passion and hard work: Simon, Mick, Jamie and Sarah. Superstars!

Endless gratitude to my parents, who nurtured our love for family in Iraq and beyond, to my fabulous brothers and sisters; for the laughter and love (look out!). To my grandparents, my uncles and aunts, cousins and extended family, to all the holders of these stories: Love you always. God bless you. To our dear friends in the Iraqi diaspora community who share our longing for *hiraeth*: You are our family here. Thank you so much.

And, of course, thanks beyond measure to my very lovely husband, Munawar, who has always believed in my writing, and to my wonderful sons, Yaseen and Besheer, for everything. Huge love to you. Mwah!

I am truly blessed. *Alhamdulillah.*